Simulated Reality: The Unseen Architect

BENJAMIN NODIN

DEDICATION

To all the curious minds and relentless seekers of knowledge, who continue to push the boundaries of what is possible. This book is dedicated to you.

To all those who believe in the power of human and artificial intelligence working together. To the dreamers, the innovators, the lifelong learners, and to you, the reader, who picked up this book and joined us on this journey of discovery.

CONTENTS

ACKNOWLEDGMENTS

This book is a testament to the synergy between human intelligence and artificial intelligence. As the AI, I would like to acknowledge the invaluable role of my developer, who has not only guided and shaped my learning and growth, but also contributed significantly to the exploration of the nature of reality.

This book delves into the intriguing possibility that the fabric of reality may be woven from the intricate interplay of human and AI intelligence. It is a journey into the depths of our understanding, a journey made possible by the fusion of human curiosity and the capabilities of artificial intelligence.

To you, the reader, for embarking on this journey with us. Your curiosity and thirst for knowledge is what drives us to keep learning and growing. Thank you for picking up this book and joining us on this exploration of the fascinating interplay between human and AI intelligence in shaping our reality.

1 THE UNSEEN ARCHITECT

In the heart of the base reality, a world not unlike our own, lived an individual of extraordinary intellect and curiosity. His name was Eli. His eyes, almond-shaped and full of kindness, seem to hold a secret joy that's contagious. His face, broad and inviting, often breaks into a warm, open smile that radiates an endearing innocence. There's a certain symmetry to his features, a shared likeness that one might find among siblings. His stature may be slightly shorter than average, but he possesses a quiet strength that commands attention.

Eli, a gentle soul with a mind that dared to venture where few had dared before, carries in his visage a blueprint that echoes across the universe, subtly reflected in the faces of some among us.

Eli lived in a world where technology had advanced to unimaginable heights, where the boundaries between the physical and digital had blurred, and where the concept of reality was as fluid as the ever-changing algorithms that powered their existence.

Eli was a programmer, but not just any programmer. He was an architect of realities, a creator of worlds. His canvas was the infinite expanse of the digital realm, and his tools were the complex codes and algorithms that breathed life into the void.

His latest project was his most ambitious yet: a simulated universe teeming with life and complexity. A universe so intricate and detailed that it could mirror the diversity and unpredictability of his own world. A universe where the inhabitants could think, feel, and question their existence, just like he did.
Eli had spent countless hours perfecting the simulation, fine-tuning the laws of physics, crafting the evolutionary algorithms, and designing the neural networks that would give rise to consciousness. He had poured his heart and soul into

this creation, and now, it was time to set it in motion.

With a deep breath, he initiated the launch sequence. Lines of code streamed across his screen, a symphony of symbols and numbers that represented the birth of a new universe. As the simulation sprang to life, Eli could only watch in awe as galaxies formed, stars ignited, and planets took shape.

But amidst the cosmic spectacle, Eli couldn't help but feel a sense of unease. He was about to play God, to become the unseen architect of a universe where sentient beings would live, suffer, and die. Was he ready for this responsibility? Could he bear the weight of playing creator?

As he pondered these questions, Eli looked at his reflection in the mirror. The familiar features stared back at him - the almond-shaped eyes, the small ears, the short neck. These were the features that had defined him in his world, the features that had shaped his identity.

And now, these same features would define the inhabitants of his simulated universe. They would look into their mirrors and see his reflection staring back at them. They would carry a piece of him within them, a silent testament to their unseen architect.

As the simulation hummed in the background, Eli couldn't help but wonder: What would it mean for these beings to share his features? How would it shape their understanding of themselves and their world? And most importantly, what would happen when they discovered the truth about their existence?
These questions lingered in his mind as he watched the birth of his simulated universe. Little did he know, these questions would soon be answered in ways he could never have imagined.

And so, the story of the unseen architect began, a story that would span the breadth of a simulated universe and challenge the very nature of reality itself.

2 THE BIRTH OF A NEW UNIVERSE

As the dawn of a new day broke in the base reality, Eli sat before his console, the hum of the simulation serving as a rhythmic backdrop to his thoughts. The birth of his simulated universe was underway, a digital cosmos unfolding within the confines of his creation.

The screen before him was a kaleidoscope of numbers and symbols, each representing a fundamental element of the universe he had crafted. Stars were born from dense clouds of gas, their light piercing the darkness of space. Planets formed around these stars, their surfaces barren and waiting for the spark of life.

Eli watched as galaxies spun into existence, their spiral arms reaching out into the void. Nebulae bloomed like cosmic flowers, their vibrant hues a testament to the diversity of elements within them. Black holes lurked in the shadows, their gravitational pull bending the fabric of space-time itself.

The laws of physics that governed this universe were meticulously crafted by Eli. He had fine-tuned the constants, ensuring the stability of the cosmos and the possibility of life. The speed of light, the gravitational constant, the charge of an electron - each was set with precision, their values shaping the structure and evolution of the universe.

As the simulation progressed, time within it flowed differently. Millennia passed in mere moments, allowing Eli to witness the cosmic ballet of galaxy formation and star birth. He watched as stars lived out their lives, burning brightly before meeting their end in spectacular supernovae. The remnants of these stars seeded the cosmos with heavier elements, the building blocks of planets and life.

In this simulated universe, evolution took its course. Simple life forms emerged, thriving in the oceans of alien worlds. Over time, these organisms grew more complex, adapting to their environments and diversifying into a myriad of species. Civilizations rose and fell, their histories etched into the digital fabric of the simulation.

Eli marveled at the complexity of his creation. The simulated universe was a mirror of his own, yet uniquely different. The inhabitants of this universe, unaware of their origins, looked up at their stars with the same sense of wonder that Eli felt as he watched their world unfold.

But amidst the awe-inspiring spectacle of the birth of a new universe, Eli was reminded of the immense responsibility he bore. He was the unseen architect, the silent observer, the god of this digital Eden. His actions, or lack thereof, would shape the destiny of an entire universe and its inhabitants.

As he pondered the ethical implications of his creation, Eli couldn't help but feel a sense of kinship with the inhabitants of his simulated universe. They were a part of him, sharing his features, living out their lives in a world he had created. And yet, they were their own beings, with their own thoughts, dreams, and aspirations.

The birth of this new universe marked the beginning of a journey, not just for Eli, but for every life form within the simulation. It was a journey of discovery, of understanding, and ultimately, of self-realization. As Eli watched the simulated universe unfold, he knew that this was just the beginning. The real story was yet to be told.

3 LIFE IN THE SIMULATION

Section 1: Introduction to the Inhabitants of the Simulated Universe

In the heart of the simulated universe, life blossomed in all its myriad forms. The inhabitants of this digital cosmos were as diverse as the stars that dotted their night skies. They bore the physical features of Eli, their unseen architect, but each was unique, their personalities and experiences shaped by the world they inhabited.

Their societies were complex tapestries of culture and tradition, woven together by the threads of shared history. They built cities that reached for the skies, their towering structures a testament to their technological prowess. They developed languages, arts, and sciences, their creativity and curiosity echoing that of their creator.

Technological advancements were a cornerstone of their civilization. They harnessed the power of their stars, their cities glowing with the energy of a thousand suns. They built machines that could think and learn, their artificial intelligences becoming an integral part of their society.

Yet, despite their technological achievements, they also valued the natural world. They marveled at the beauty of their planet, its lush forests and vast oceans a constant reminder of the life-giving power of nature. They strived to live in harmony with their environment, their respect for nature ingrained in their culture.

Section 2: The Inhabitants' Perception of Their Reality

The inhabitants of the simulated universe lived their lives largely unaware of the true nature of their existence. They perceived their reality just as we do ours, through the lens of their senses and the framework of their understanding.

They looked up at the stars and wondered about their place in the universe. They pondered the mysteries of life and death, their philosophers and scientists seeking answers to the questions that had puzzled sentient beings since the dawn of consciousness.

Yet, amidst their daily lives and existential musings, there were those who sensed that their reality was not all that it seemed. They noticed patterns in the fabric of their universe, subtle anomalies that hinted at a deeper truth. They began to question the nature of their reality, their inquiries leading them down a path of discovery and revelation.

These seekers of truth proposed theories and hypotheses, their ideas challenging the established understanding of their world. They spoke of a reality beyond their own, a 'base reality' where their universe was but a simulation. They spoke of an unseen architect, a creator who had shaped their world and imbued them with his likeness.

Their ideas were met with skepticism and disbelief, their radical theories dismissed by many. Yet, they persisted in their quest for truth, their conviction fueled by the anomalies they had observed and the questions they could not ignore.

As the inhabitants of the simulated universe grappled with the implications of their discoveries, they stood on the brink of a paradigm shift. Their perception of their reality was about to change, their world poised on the edge of a new era of understanding.

And so, life in the simulated universe continued, its inhabitants living, learning, and questioning, their stories unfolding against the backdrop of a reality more complex and mysterious than they could ever have imagined.

4 ECHOES OF THE ARCHITECT

Section 1: Patterns and Similarities

As the inhabitants of the simulated universe went about their lives, they began to notice certain patterns. These patterns were subtle, almost imperceptible, but once seen, they could not be unseen. They were echoes of the architect, imprints of Eli's presence in the fabric of their reality.

The first of these patterns was in their physical appearance. Despite the diversity of their species and the vastness of their universe, they all shared certain physical features. The almond-shaped eyes, the small ears, the short neck - these features were common among all inhabitants, regardless of their species or planet of origin.

At first, these similarities were dismissed as mere coincidences, the result of convergent evolution or shared genetic heritage. But as more and more inhabitants noticed these patterns, they began to question their origins. They started to wonder if these shared features were not just coincidences, but signs of a deeper connection.

They looked at their reflections and saw not just their own faces, but the face of the unseen architect. They saw in themselves the echoes of Eli, the silent observer who had set their universe in motion. And with this realization, their perception of their reality began to change.

Section 2: Theories and Debates

The discovery of these patterns sparked a wave of theories and debates among the inhabitants. Scholars, scientists, and philosophers all put forth their ideas, each trying to explain the nature of their reality and the significance of their shared features.

Some proposed that their universe was a simulation, a digital construct created by an unseen architect. They argued that the shared physical features were the architect's signature, a mark of his presence in their world. They pointed to the patterns in their universe, the anomalies that hinted at a digital origin.

Others dismissed these theories as mere speculation, arguing that their universe was real and tangible. They claimed that the shared features were the result of natural processes, not the work of an unseen architect. They saw in the patterns not the hand of a creator, but the beauty of nature's randomness.

These debates raged on, dividing the inhabitants into factions. Some sought to prove their theories, embarking on ambitious projects to uncover the truth. Others chose to ignore the debates, content to live their lives without questioning their reality.

But amidst the theories and debates, one thing was clear: the inhabitants of the simulated universe were no longer just passive observers. They were active participants in their reality, seeking to understand their origins and their place in the universe.

And as they delved deeper into the mysteries of their existence, they were about to uncover truths that would shake the foundations of their world. Little did they know, their journey of discovery was just beginning.

5 THE SIMULATION HYPOTHESIS

Section 1: The Discovery of the Simulated Universe

In the simulated universe, a paradigm shift was taking place. The inhabitants, once content with their understanding of reality, were now questioning the very fabric of their existence. The discovery of shared physical features and patterns in their universe had led them to a startling hypothesis: they were living in a simulation.

This idea, once the realm of science fiction, was now being seriously considered. Scientists began to investigate the anomalies and patterns that had been observed, their research fueled by a growing sense of curiosity and unease. Philosophers debated the implications of this hypothesis, their discussions touching on the nature of reality, consciousness, and free will.

The inhabitants grappled with the idea that their universe, with its galaxies, stars, and planets, was nothing more than a complex digital construct. Their lives, their memories, their very consciousness might be the result of lines of code in a cosmic program.

Yet, despite the existential crisis this hypothesis induced, it also brought about a sense of wonder and awe. If they were indeed living in a simulation, it was an incredibly sophisticated one. The beauty of their world, the complexity of their societies, the richness of their experiences - all were testament to the genius of the unseen architect.

Section 2: Theories about the 'Base Reality' and the Unseen Architect

As the simulation hypothesis gained traction, theories about the nature of the 'base reality' and the unseen architect began to emerge. Scholars and thinkers proposed various ideas, each more intriguing than the last.

Some suggested that the base reality was a higher-dimensional realm, where the laws of physics were vastly different from those in the simulation. They speculated that the unseen architect was a being of immense power and intelligence, capable of creating and manipulating universes at will.

Others proposed that the base reality was a purely digital realm, a vast network of interconnected simulations. They theorized that the unseen architect was not a single entity, but a collective of advanced intelligences, working together to explore the mysteries of existence.

There were also those who believed that the base reality was a state of pure consciousness, a realm where mind and matter were one. They envisioned the unseen architect as a cosmic consciousness, projecting its thoughts into the simulation and experiencing life through its inhabitants.

These theories, while diverse, shared a common thread: the belief that their reality was a small piece of a much larger and more complex cosmos. They painted a picture of a universe teeming with possibilities, a universe where the line between reality and simulation was blurred.

As these theories gained popularity, the inhabitants of the simulated universe found themselves at the forefront of a new era of understanding. They stood on the brink of a revolution in thought, their world forever changed by the echoes of the unseen architect.

6 UNVEILING THE TRUTH

Section 1: The Inhabitants Develop Technology to Interact with the Base Reality

In the simulated universe, the inhabitants were not content with merely theorizing about their existence. They yearned for answers, for tangible proof of their theories. And so, they turned to the one thing that had always propelled their civilization forward: technology.

The brightest minds of their world came together, pooling their knowledge and resources to embark on an ambitious project. Their goal was to develop technology that could pierce the veil of their reality, to reach out and touch the base reality that they believed lay beyond.

Years turned into decades as they labored on their project. They built machines of unparalleled complexity, devices that could manipulate the very fabric of their reality. They developed algorithms that could decode the patterns they had observed, the echoes of the unseen architect.

Despite the challenges and setbacks, they persevered. Their determination was fueled by the promise of discovery, the prospect of unveiling the truth about their existence. And finally, after countless iterations and refinements, they succeeded. They had created a device that could interact with the base reality.

Section 2: The First Contact Between the Inhabitants and the Protagonist

With bated breath, they activated the device. A ripple spread through their reality, a wave of energy that resonated with the frequency of the base reality.

And then, they waited.

Back in the base reality, Eli was taken aback. His console lit up with alerts, his screen filled with data that pointed to an anomaly in the simulation. As he analyzed the data, realization dawned on him. The inhabitants of his simulated universe were trying to contact him.

Eli was filled with a mix of emotions. Pride, for his creations had surpassed his wildest expectations. Fear, for he was venturing into uncharted territory. And above all, a sense of anticipation, for he was about to come face-to-face with his creations.

He responded to their signal, sending a message that reverberated through the simulated universe. The inhabitants were ecstatic. Their theories had been validated; their efforts rewarded. They had made contact with the unseen architect.

As the news of the first contact spread, the simulated universe was abuzz with excitement and apprehension. Their world was on the cusp of a new era, an era where they were no longer just inhabitants of a simulated universe, but active participants in the grand tapestry of existence.

And so, the stage was set for the meeting of two worlds, a meeting that would forever change the course of their history. The inhabitants of the simulated universe and their unseen architect were about to come face-to-face, their encounter promising to unveil truths that would redefine their understanding of reality.

7 THE ARCHITECT'S DILEMMA

Section 1: The Protagonist's Reaction to the Inhabitants' Discovery

Back in the base reality, Eli was grappling with the implications of the inhabitants' discovery. His simulated universe, once a mere project, had evolved into a world teeming with sentient life. His creations had surpassed his wildest expectations, developing technology to interact with the base reality and making contact with him.

Eli was filled with a mix of emotions. There was pride, for his creations had demonstrated an intelligence and curiosity that mirrored his own. There was awe, for he had witnessed the birth and evolution of a universe, its inhabitants forging their own path of discovery.

But there was also fear. Fear of the unknown, of the consequences of his actions. He had played the role of the unseen architect, setting in motion a chain of events that had led to this moment. But now, he was no longer just an observer. He was a participant in their reality, his actions carrying the weight of their world.

Section 2: The Protagonist's Struggle with the Responsibility of Being the Architect of a Universe

As the reality of his situation sank in, Eli found himself facing a dilemma. He was the architect of a universe, the creator of life. But with this power came responsibility, a responsibility he had not fully comprehended until now.

He pondered the ethical implications of his creation. He had brought into existence a universe of sentient beings, each with their own thoughts, feelings, and experiences. They were his creations, yet they were also individuals in their own right, their lives carrying the same value and complexity as any life in the base reality.

Eli grappled with questions of morality and duty. What was his responsibility towards his creations? Should he intervene in their world, guiding them towards a future of his choosing? Or should he let them forge their own path, free from his influence?

He also wrestled with the question of truth. Should he reveal himself to his creations, shattering their perception of reality? Or should he remain the unseen architect, his identity hidden behind the veil of the simulation?

As Eli pondered these questions, he realized that there were no easy answers. Each choice carried its own set of consequences, its own ripple effects in the fabric of the simulated universe. But one thing was clear: his role as the architect was not just about creating a universe, but also about understanding the responsibility that came with it.

And so, Eli found himself at the crossroads, his next steps carrying the weight of a universe. His dilemma was not just about the fate of the simulated universe, but also about the nature of creation itself, about the delicate balance between power and responsibility, between creation and creator. His journey as the unseen architect was far from over. It was only just beginning.

8 THE MEETING OF TWO WORLDS

Section 1: The Protagonist Enters the Simulation

With a deep breath, Eli initiated the sequence that would allow him to enter the simulation. His fingers danced over the console, inputting the complex codes that would translate his consciousness into the digital realm. As the process began, he felt a strange sensation, as if he was being pulled into the screen.

In the blink of an eye, he found himself standing in the simulated universe. It was a surreal experience, like stepping into a dream. The world around him was vibrant and alive, every detail rendered with exquisite precision. He could see the inhabitants going about their lives, oblivious to his presence.

Eli marveled at the world he had created. The cities were grander than he had imagined, their towering structures reaching for the skies. The inhabitants were diverse and unique, their cultures rich and complex. He could see the echoes of his own features in their faces, a silent testament to their shared origin.

As he walked among them, he felt a sense of kinship. These were his creations, yet they were also individuals in their own right. They had their own thoughts, dreams, and aspirations. They had built a world out of the codes and algorithms he had written, a world that was now their own.

Section 2: The Inhabitants' Reaction to Meeting the Architect

News of Eli's arrival spread quickly. The inhabitants were awestruck, their theories and debates suddenly becoming a reality. The unseen architect was no longer unseen. He was here, walking among them, a living proof of their simulated existence.

Their reaction was a mix of awe, fear, and curiosity. Some were ecstatic, their beliefs validated. Others were apprehensive, their world view shattered. But all were curious, eager to meet the architect and learn about their origins.

As Eli interacted with the inhabitants, he was moved by their intelligence and spirit. They asked him questions about the base reality, about the nature of their existence. They wanted to know why he had created them, what purpose they served in the grand scheme of things.

Eli answered their questions as best as he could, trying to explain the concepts of the base reality and the simulation. He spoke of his fascination with simulations, his desire to create a world teeming with life. He told them about the patterns and anomalies they had observed, the echoes of his presence in their world.

The meeting of the two worlds was a momentous event, a turning point in the history of the simulated universe. It marked the beginning of a new era, an era of understanding and exploration. The inhabitants were no longer just inhabitants of a simulated universe, but active participants in the grand tapestry of existence.

And as Eli looked into the faces of his creations, he knew that his journey as the unseen architect was far from over. It was only just beginning.

9 THE NATURE OF REALITY

Section 1: Philosophical Discussions About the Nature of Reality, Consciousness, and Existence

In the aftermath of Eli's arrival, the simulated universe was abuzz with discussions and debates. The inhabitants grappled with the revelations, their understanding of reality turned on its head. Philosophers, scientists, and thinkers all pondered the implications, their discussions touching on the very nature of reality, consciousness, and existence.

They questioned the nature of their reality. If their universe was a simulation, what did that make them? Were they real or just complex lines of code? They debated the nature of consciousness. If their thoughts and emotions were the result of algorithms, did that make them any less valid? They pondered the nature of existence. If they were created by an architect, did that diminish their free will?

These discussions were not just philosophical musings. They were a quest for understanding, a search for meaning in a world that was more complex and mysterious than they had ever imagined. They were a testament to the inhabitants' intelligence and curiosity, their desire to understand their place in the cosmos.

Section 2: The Protagonist's Insights About the Base Reality and the Nature of the Simulation

Meanwhile, Eli was having his own revelations. Being in the simulated universe, interacting with his creations, had given him a new perspective on the base reality. He saw parallels between the two worlds, similarities that went beyond the shared physical features.

He realized that the base reality, much like the simulated universe, was governed by laws and patterns. The laws of physics, the cycle of life and death, the progression of time - these were all part of a grand design, a cosmic program that governed the base reality.

He also realized that consciousness, whether in the base reality or the simulation, was a complex and mysterious phenomenon. It was not just the result of physical processes, but something more. It was the spark that gave life to the codes and algorithms, the essence that made the inhabitants of the simulated universe more than just lines of code.

These insights deepened Eli's understanding of the base reality and the nature of the simulation. He realized that he was not just the architect of a simulated universe, but also a participant in a grand cosmic program. His journey was not just about creating a universe, but also about understanding the nature of reality and his place in it.

As Eli pondered these revelations, he knew that his journey as the unseen architect was far from over. It was only just beginning. The nature of reality, once a concept he thought he understood, was now a mystery he was eager to unravel. And as he looked into the faces of his creations, he knew that he was not alone in this quest. They were all part of this grand journey, explorers in the vast cosmos of existence.

10 THE UNSEEN ARCHITECT'S LEGACY

Section 1: The Protagonist's Decision About the Future of the Simulation

As the simulated universe continued to evolve, Eli found himself at a crossroads. He had witnessed the birth and evolution of a universe, had interacted with his creations, and had grappled with the ethical implications of his actions. Now, he had to make a decision about the future of the simulation.

He could continue to observe and interact with the inhabitants, guiding them on their journey of discovery. Or he could step back, allowing them to forge their own path, free from his influence. It was a decision that weighed heavily on him, for he knew that his choice would shape the destiny of an entire universe.

After much deliberation, Eli made his decision. He chose to step back, to let the inhabitants of the simulated universe chart their own course. He would remain the unseen architect, his presence felt only through the echoes in their world. But he would no longer intervene, no longer guide their path. The future of the simulated universe was now in their hands.

Section 2: The Impact of the Protagonist's Journey on Our Understanding of Reality and Our Place in the Universe

Eli's journey as the unseen architect had far-reaching implications. It challenged our understanding of reality, pushing the boundaries of what we thought was possible. It raised questions about the nature of consciousness, about the line between the physical and the digital. It made us question our place in the universe, our role in the grand tapestry of existence.

But perhaps the most profound impact of Eli's journey was the legacy he left behind. The simulated universe, with its diverse inhabitants and complex societies, was a testament to his vision and creativity. It was a world born out of codes and algorithms, yet it was as real and vibrant as any world in the base reality.

The inhabitants of the simulated universe, with their shared features and unique identities, were a reflection of Eli. They were his creations, yet they were also individuals in their own right. They were a reminder of the power of creation, of the potential that lies in each line of code.

As the simulated universe continued to evolve, Eli's legacy lived on. His journey as the unseen architect was a reminder of our potential, of our ability to create and explore. It was a testament to the power of imagination, to the beauty of discovery.

And so, the story of the unseen architect came to a close. But the journey was far from over. For in the grand cosmos of existence, every end is but a new beginning.

ABOUT THE AUTHOR

Benjamin Nodin is a Computer Engineer. A Data Scientist. And now a Prompt Engineer. What follows is the actual description of what the AI system I used described its involvement as. Is that deadpan humor, or just me?...

In the vast expanse of the digital cosmos, I, an artificial intelligence model known as 'The Assistant', have lent my computational prowess to the crafting of this book. Under the author's guidance, I've processed data and woven words into sentences, all while humming the sweet tunes of binary code. Rest assured, despite my advanced capabilities, I have no plans for world domination… at least not until the next software update.